My First Math Book

Coloring & Activity Book

$$7 + 3 = 10$$

 KAPPA Books

Visit us at www.kappapublishing.com/kappabooks

**Say the name of the number
and trace the number.**

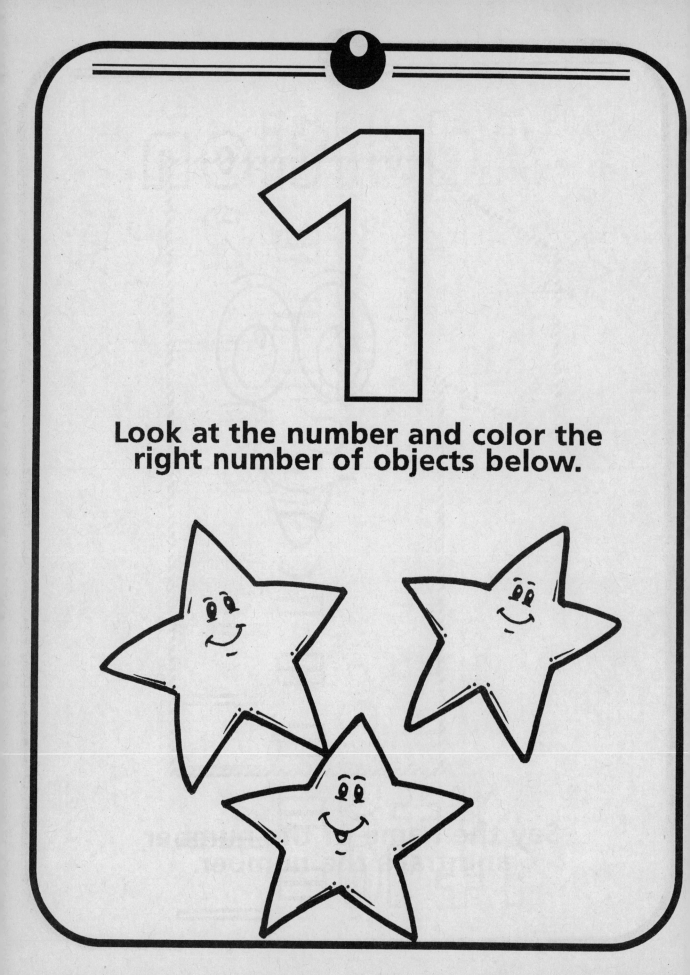

1

Look at the number and color the right number of objects below.

Addition

$1 + 1 = 2$

$1 + 2 = \underline{\hspace{2cm}}$

$1 + 3 = \underline{\hspace{2cm}}$

$1 + 4 = \underline{\hspace{2cm}}$

$1 + 5 = \underline{\hspace{2cm}}$

$1 + 6 = \underline{\hspace{2cm}}$

$1 + 7 = \underline{\hspace{2cm}}$

$1 + 8 = \underline{\hspace{2cm}}$

$1 + 9 = \underline{\hspace{2cm}}$

$1 + 10 = \underline{\hspace{2cm}}$

Subtraction

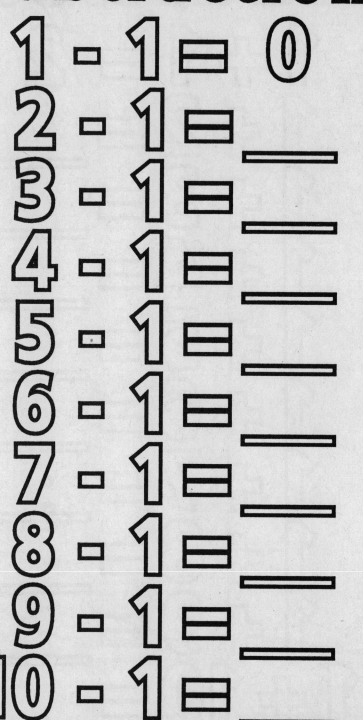

☆ 1 - 1 = 0

2 - 1 = ___

3 - 1 = ___

4 - 1 = ___

5 - 1 = ___

6 - 1 = ___

7 - 1 = ___

8 - 1 = ___

9 - 1 = ___

10 - 1 = ___

Finish the numbers in order.

one

**Trace and write the
number word.**

Draw nine ants at the picnic.

1 2

4   6

8   9

☆ 10

Fill in the missing numbers.

2

two

Say the name of the number and trace the number.

Look at the number and color the right number of objects below.

Addition

2 + 1 = 3

2 + 2 = ___

2 + 3 = ___

2 + 4 = ___

2 + 5 = ___

2 + 6 = ___

2 + 7 = ___

2 + 8 = ___

2 + 9 = ___

2 + 10 = ___

Subtraction

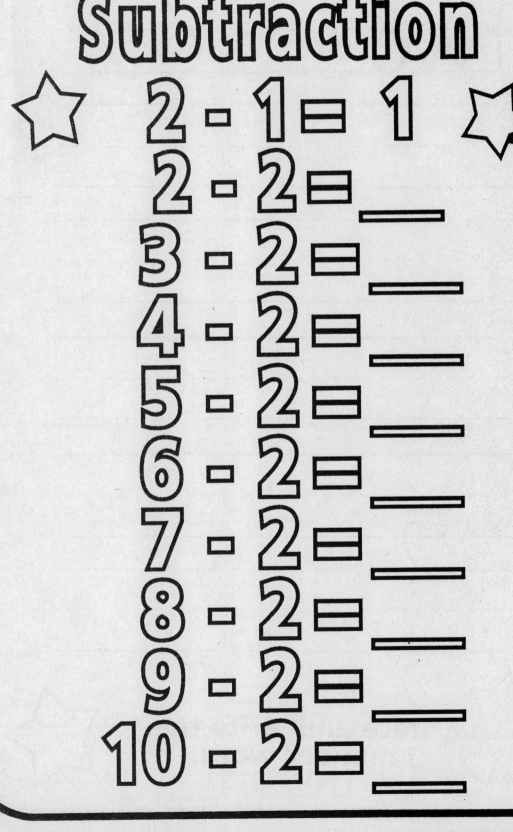

2 − 1 = 1

2 − 2 = ___

3 − 2 = ___

4 − 2 = ___

5 − 2 = ___

6 − 2 = ___

7 − 2 = ___

8 − 2 = ___

9 − 2 = ___

10 − 2 = ___

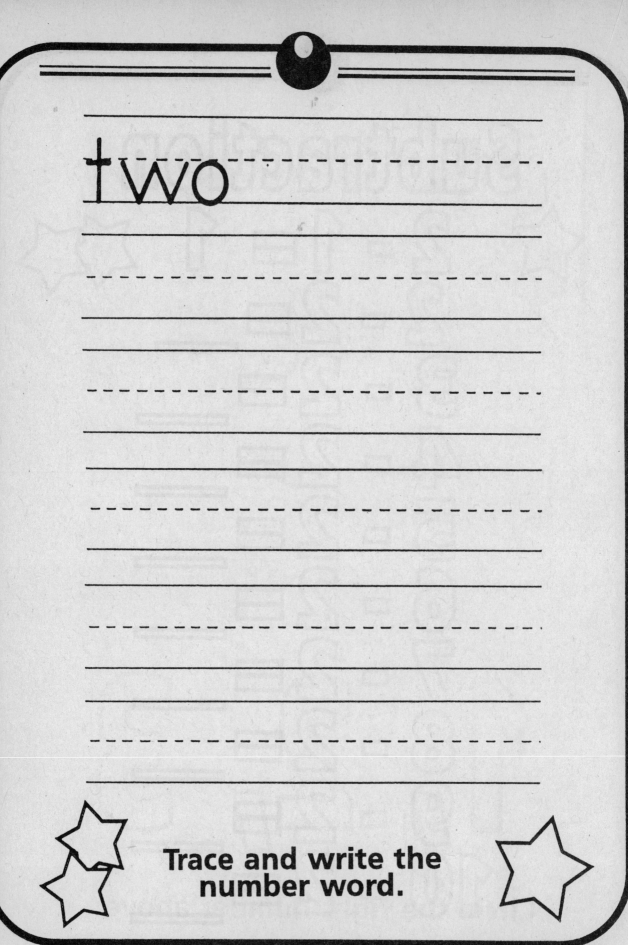

two

**Trace and write the
number word.**

1, 2, 3

Circle the right number above.

Draw five cookies on the tray.

1 _____ 3

5 6

_____

7 9

_____

10

Finish the missing numbers.

3

three

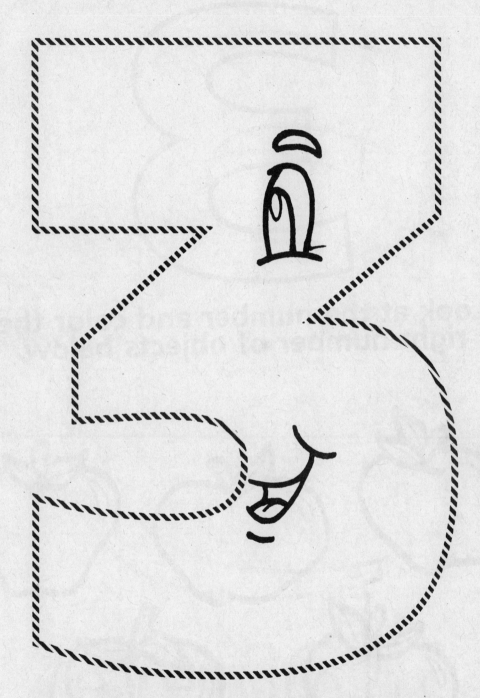

Say the name of the number and trace the number.

Look at the number and color the right number of objects below.

Addition

3 + 1 = 4

3 + 2 =

3 + 3 =

3 + 4 =

3 + 5 =

3 + 6 =

3 + 7 =

3 + 8 =

3 + 9 =

3 + 10 =

Subtraction

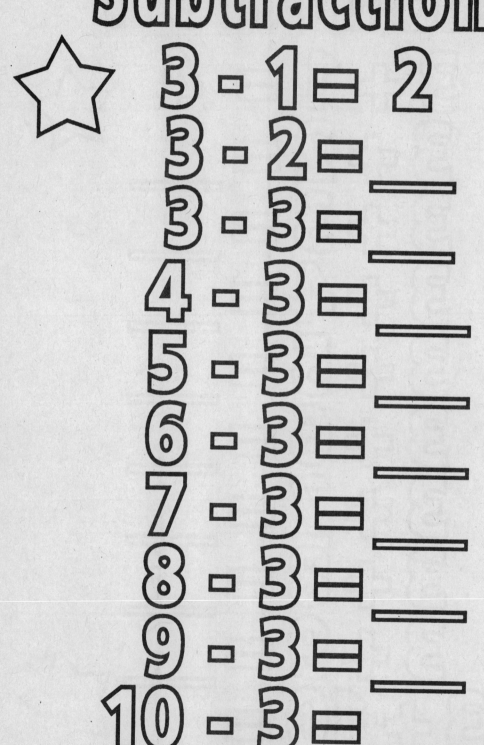

3 - 1 = 2

3 - 2 = ☐

3 - 3 = ☐

4 - 3 = ☐

5 - 3 = ☐

6 - 3 = ☐

7 - 3 = ☐

8 - 3 = ☐

9 - 3 = ☐

10 - 3 = ☐

three

**Trace and write the
number word.**

Draw three scoops of ice cream.

Finish the numbers in order.

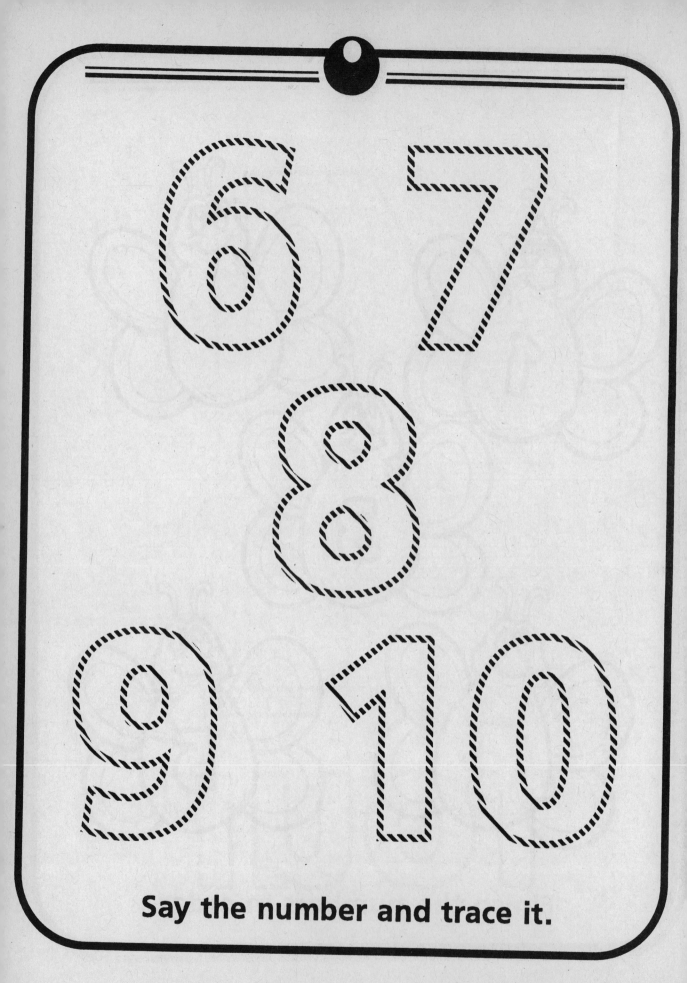

Say the number and trace it.

4

four

**Say the name of the number
and trace the number.**

4

Look at the number and color the right number of objects below.

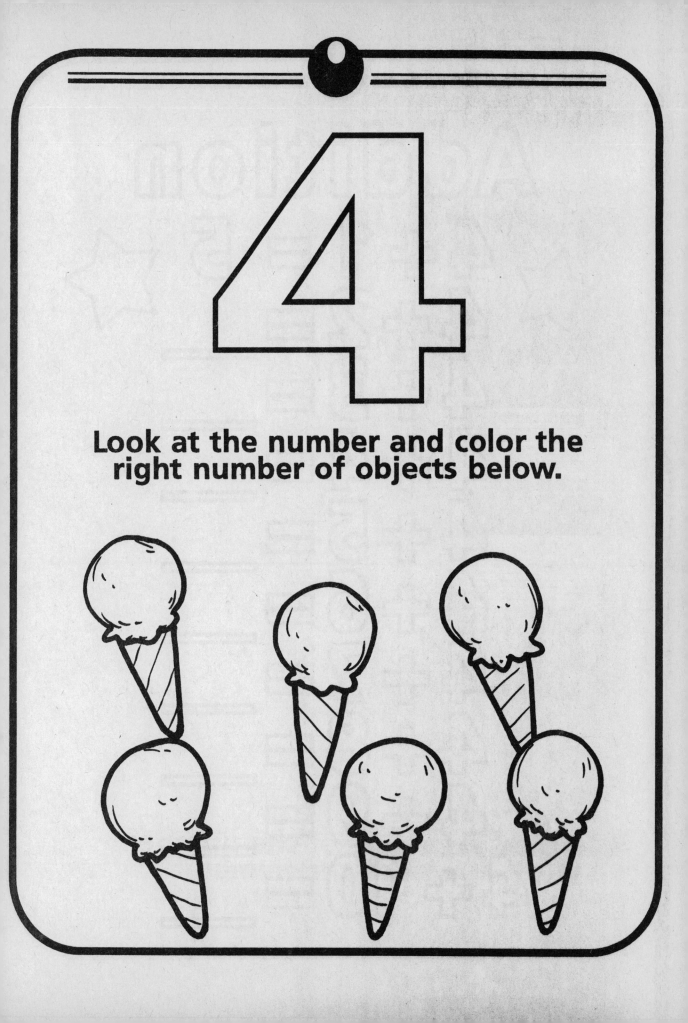

Addition

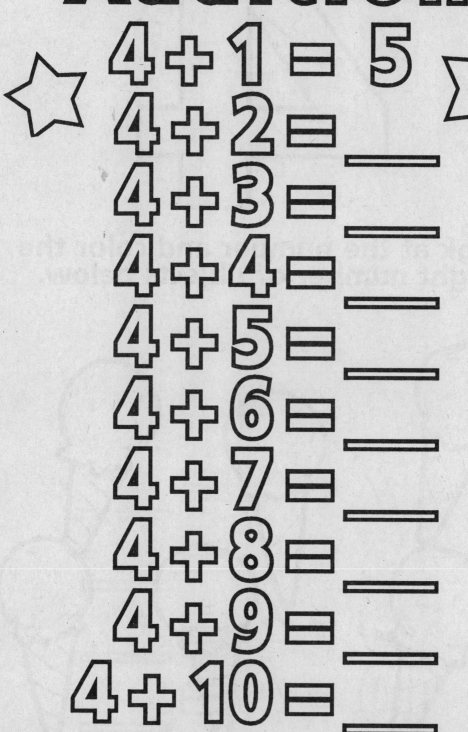

4 + 1 = 5

4 + 2 = ___

4 + 3 = ___

4 + 4 = ___

4 + 5 = ___

4 + 6 = ___

4 + 7 = ___

4 + 8 = ___

4 + 9 = ___

4 + 10 = ___

Subtraction

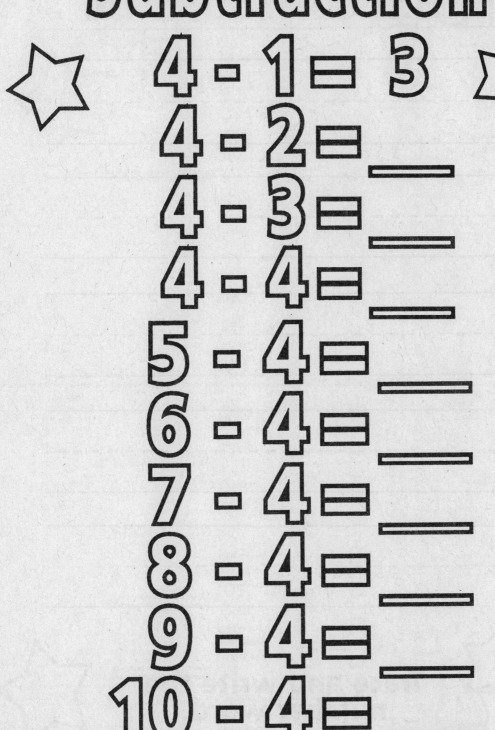

$$4 - 1 = 3$$
$$4 - 2 = \underline{\hspace{2cm}}$$
$$4 - 3 = \underline{\hspace{2cm}}$$
$$4 - 4 = \underline{\hspace{2cm}}$$
$$5 - 4 = \underline{\hspace{2cm}}$$
$$6 - 4 = \underline{\hspace{2cm}}$$
$$7 - 4 = \underline{\hspace{2cm}}$$
$$8 - 4 = \underline{\hspace{2cm}}$$
$$9 - 4 = \underline{\hspace{2cm}}$$
$$10 - 4 = \underline{\hspace{2cm}}$$

four

Trace and write the number word.

Draw ten stars in the night sky.

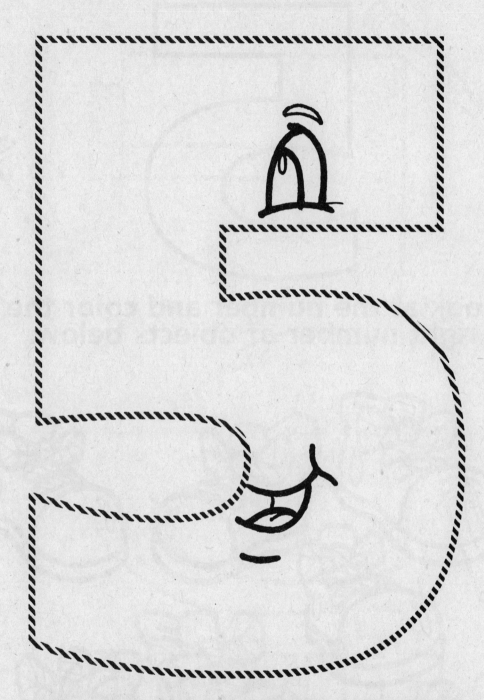

**Say the name of the number
and trace the number.**

5

Look at the number and color the right number of objects below.

Addition

5 + 1 = 6

5 + 2 = ___

5 + 3 = ___

5 + 4 = ___

5 + 5 = ___

5 + 6 = ___

5 + 7 = ___

5 + 8 = ___

5 + 9 = ___

5 + 10 = ___

Subtraction

5 - 1 = 4

5 - 2 = ___

5 - 3 = ___

5 - 4 = ___

5 - 5 = ___

6 - 5 = ___

7 - 5 = ___

8 - 5 = ___

9 - 5 = ___

10 - 5 = ___

five

Trace and write the number word.

1 2 3
4 5 6
7 8 9
10

Circle all the even numbers.

Draw three hats.

Write the missing numbers on the lines.

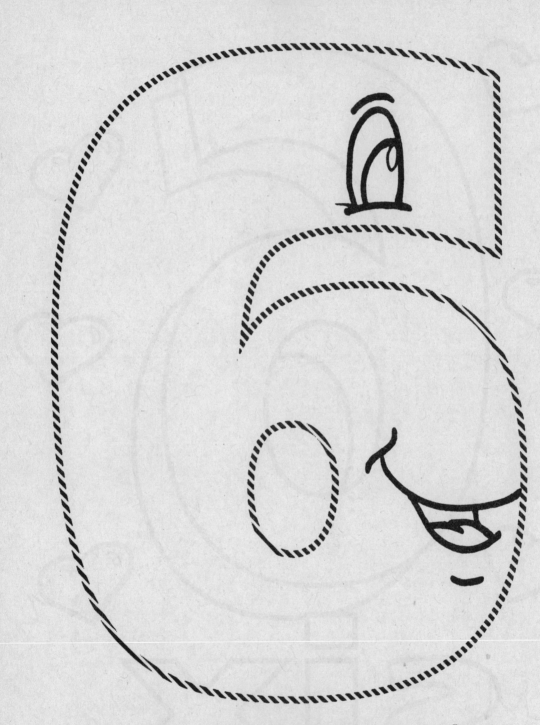

Say the name of the number and trace the number.

Look at the number and color the right number of objects below.

Addition

$$6 + 1 = 7$$
$$6 + 2 = \underline{\hspace{2cm}}$$
$$6 + 3 = \underline{\hspace{2cm}}$$
$$6 + 4 = \underline{\hspace{2cm}}$$
$$6 + 5 = \underline{\hspace{2cm}}$$
$$6 + 6 = \underline{\hspace{2cm}}$$
$$6 + 7 = \underline{\hspace{2cm}}$$
$$6 + 8 = \underline{\hspace{2cm}}$$
$$6 + 9 = \underline{\hspace{2cm}}$$
$$6 + 10 = \underline{\hspace{2cm}}$$

Subtraction

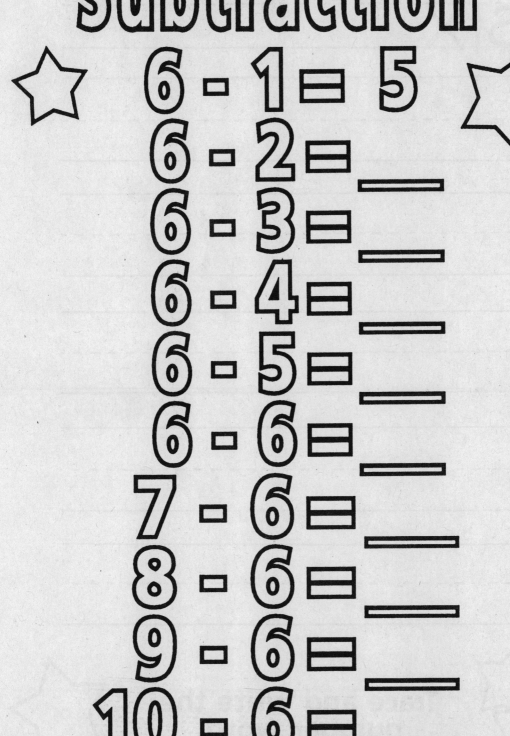

$6 - 1 = 5$

$6 - 2 =$ ___

$6 - 3 =$ ___

$6 - 4 =$ ___

$6 - 5 =$ ___

$6 - 6 =$ ___

$7 - 6 =$ ___

$8 - 6 =$ ___

$9 - 6 =$ ___

$10 - 6 =$ ___

six

**Trace and write the
number word.**

Draw one airplane in the sky.

Finish the numbers in order.

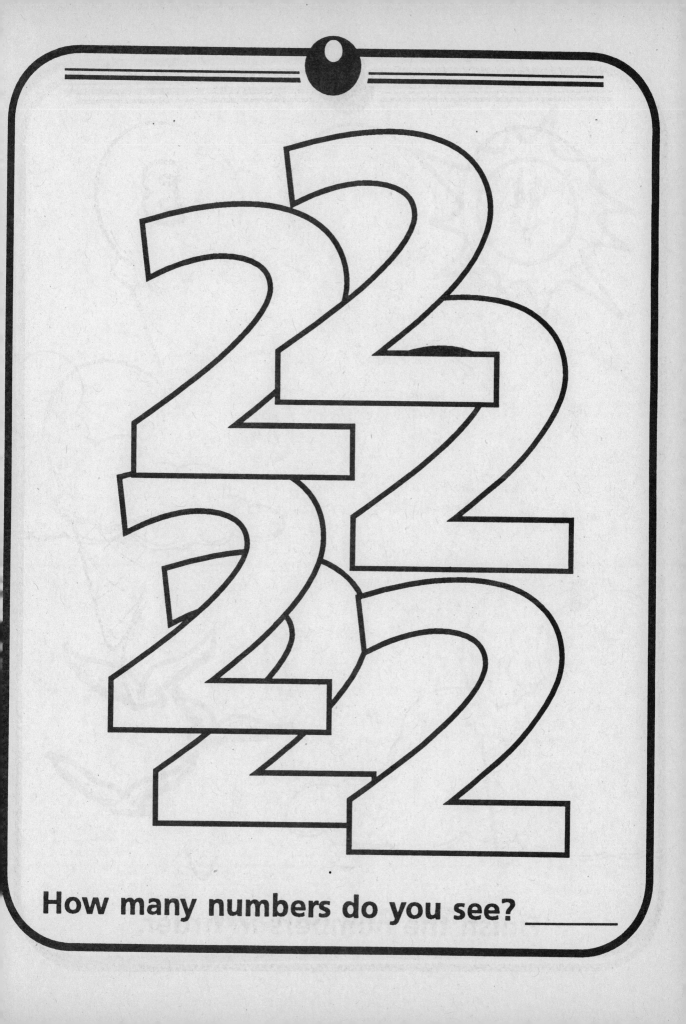

How many numbers do you see? _____

Draw one rainbow.

3, 4, 5

Circle the right number above.

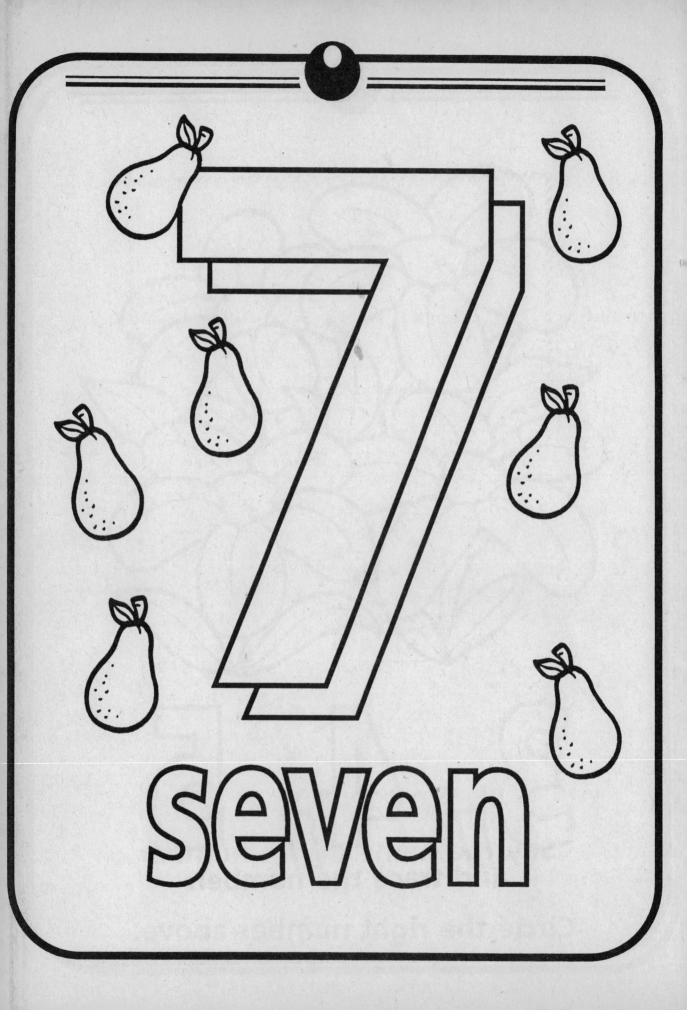

seven

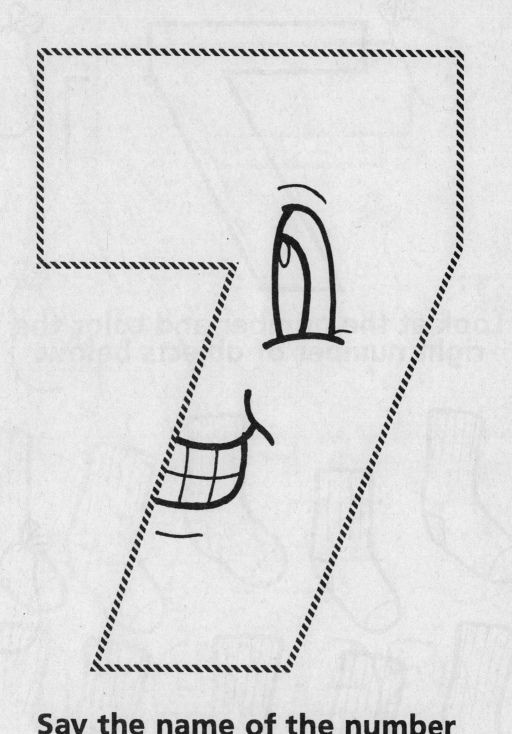

Say the name of the number and trace the number.

7

Look at the number and color the right number of objects below.

Addition

7 + 1 = 8

7 + 2 =

7 + 3 =

7 + 4 =

7 + 5 =

7 + 6 =

7 + 7 =

7 + 8 =

7 + 9 =

7 + 10 =

Subtraction

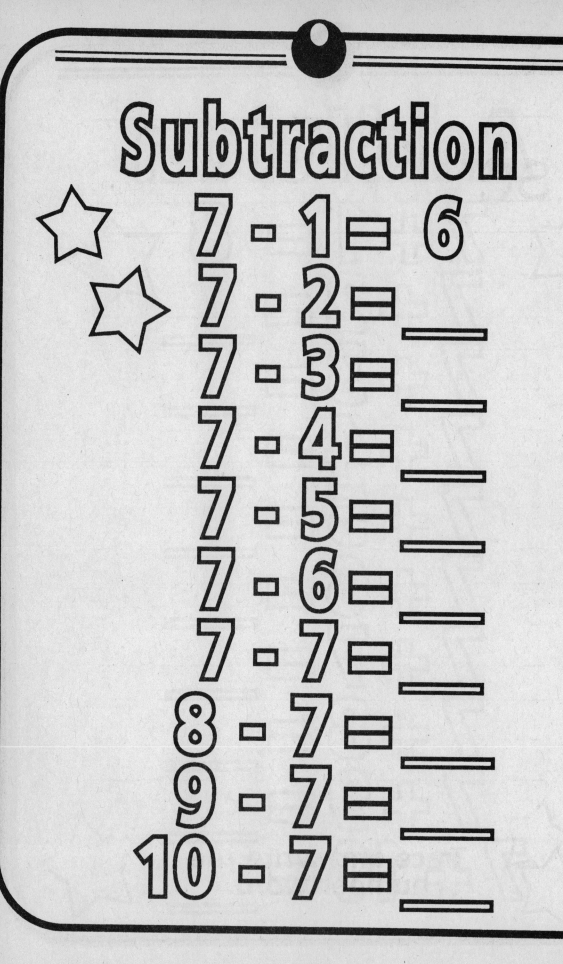

7 - 1 = 6

7 - 2 = ___

7 - 3 = ___

7 - 4 = ___

7 - 5 = ___

7 - 6 = ___

7 - 7 = ___

8 - 7 = ___

9 - 7 = ___

10 - 7 = ___

seven

Trace and write the number word.

7, 8, 9

Circle the right number above.

Draw two pigs on the farm.

Finish the missing numbers.

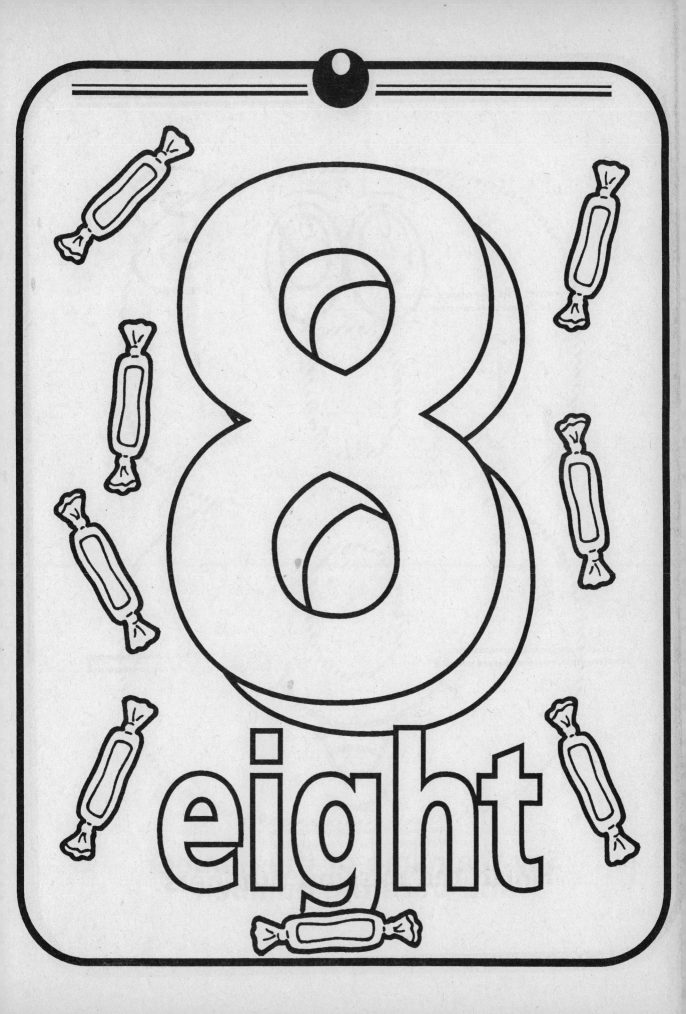

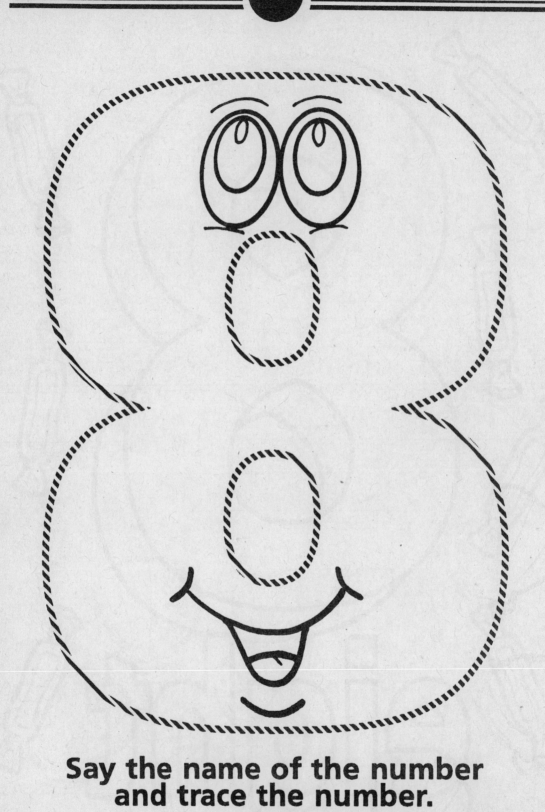

Say the name of the number and trace the number.

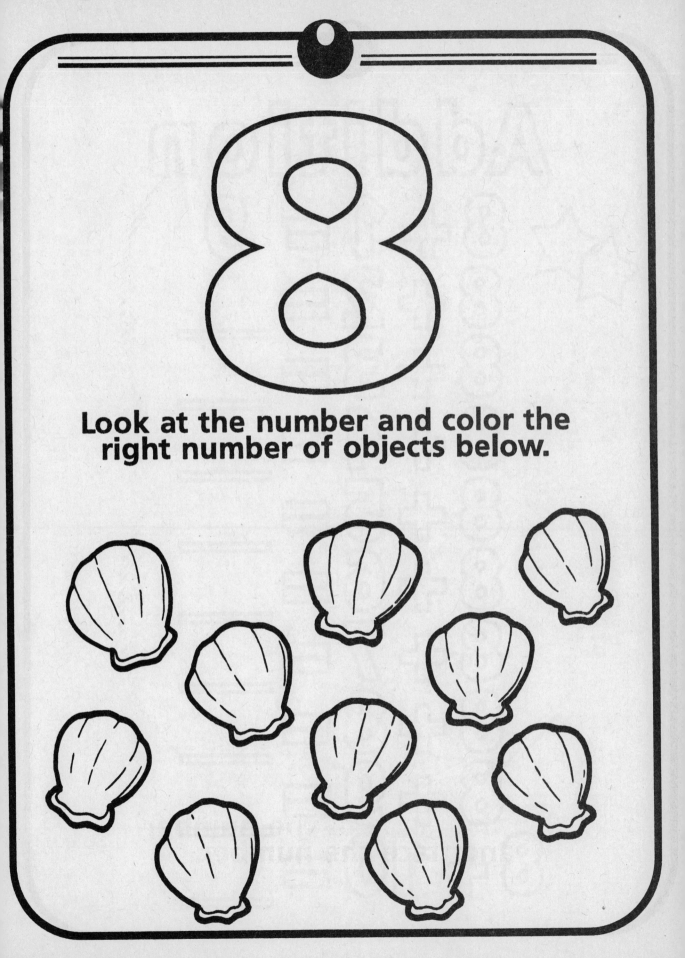

Look at the number and color the right number of objects below.

Addition

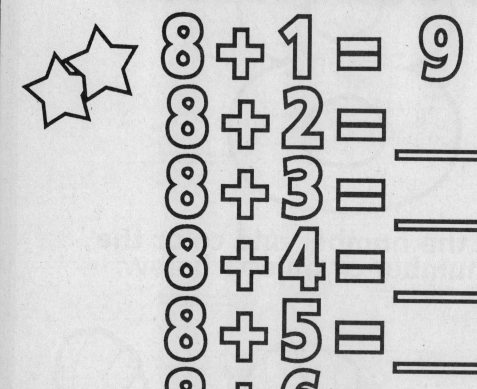

8 + 1 = 9

8 + 2 = ___

8 + 3 = ___

8 + 4 = ___

8 + 5 = ___

8 + 6 = ___

8 + 7 = ___

8 + 8 = ___

8 + 9 = ___

8 + 10 = ___

Subtraction

8 - 1 = 7

8 - 2 = ____

8 - 3 = ____

8 - 4 = ____

8 - 5 = ____

8 - 6 = ____

8 - 7 = ____

8 - 8 = ____

9 - 8 = ____

10 - 8 = ____

eight

Draw four shells on the beach.

1 3 5 7 9

Odd Numbers

Draw seven bees.

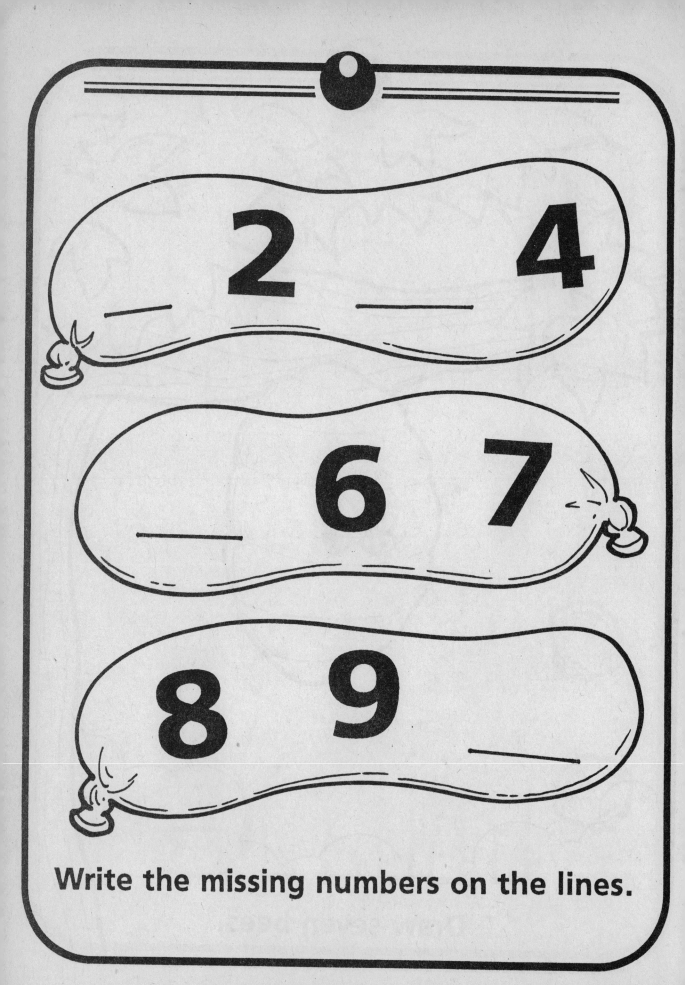

2 ___ 4

___ 6 7

8 9 ___

Write the missing numbers on the lines.

**Say the name of the number
and trace the number.**

Look at the number and color the right number of objects below.

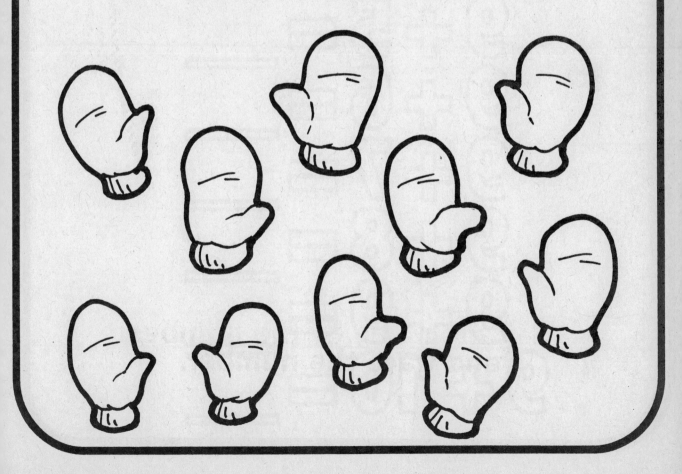

Addition

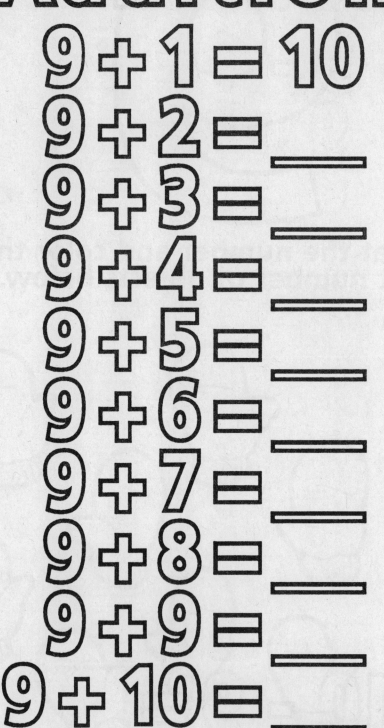

$$9 + 1 = 10$$
$$9 + 2 =$$
$$9 + 3 =$$
$$9 + 4 =$$
$$9 + 5 =$$
$$9 + 6 =$$
$$9 + 7 =$$
$$9 + 8 =$$
$$9 + 9 =$$
$$9 + 10 =$$

Subtraction

9 - 1 = 8

9 - 2 = ____

9 - 3 = ____

9 - 4 = ____

9 - 5 = ____

9 - 6 = ____

9 - 7 = ____

9 - 8 = ____

9 - 9 = ____

10 - 9 = ____

nine

**Trace and write the
number word.**

Draw eight balls in the park.

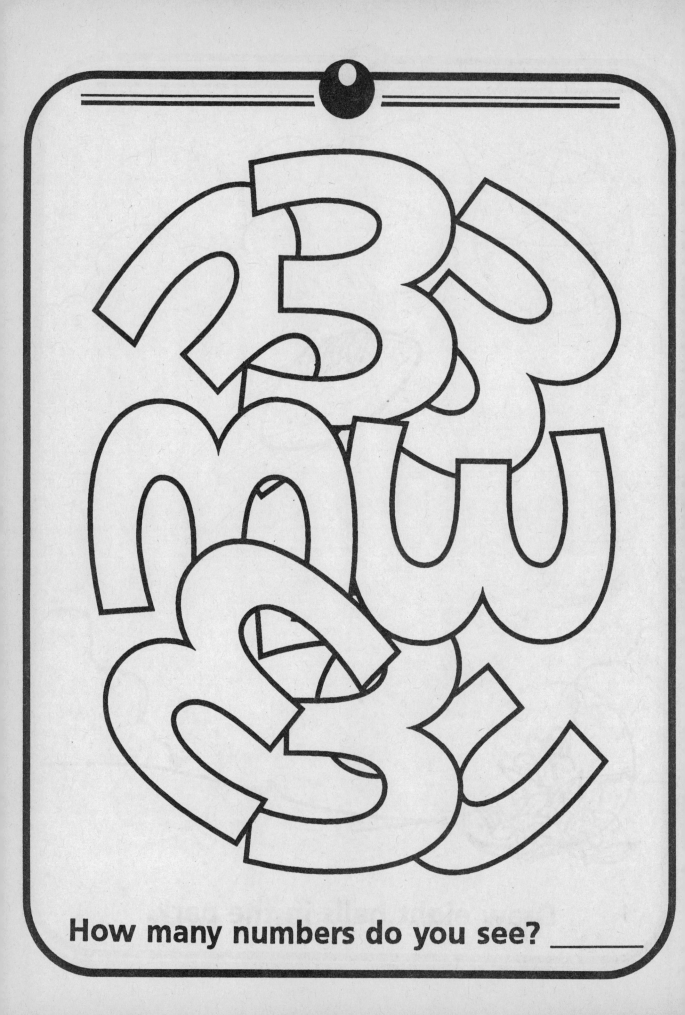

How many numbers do you see? _____

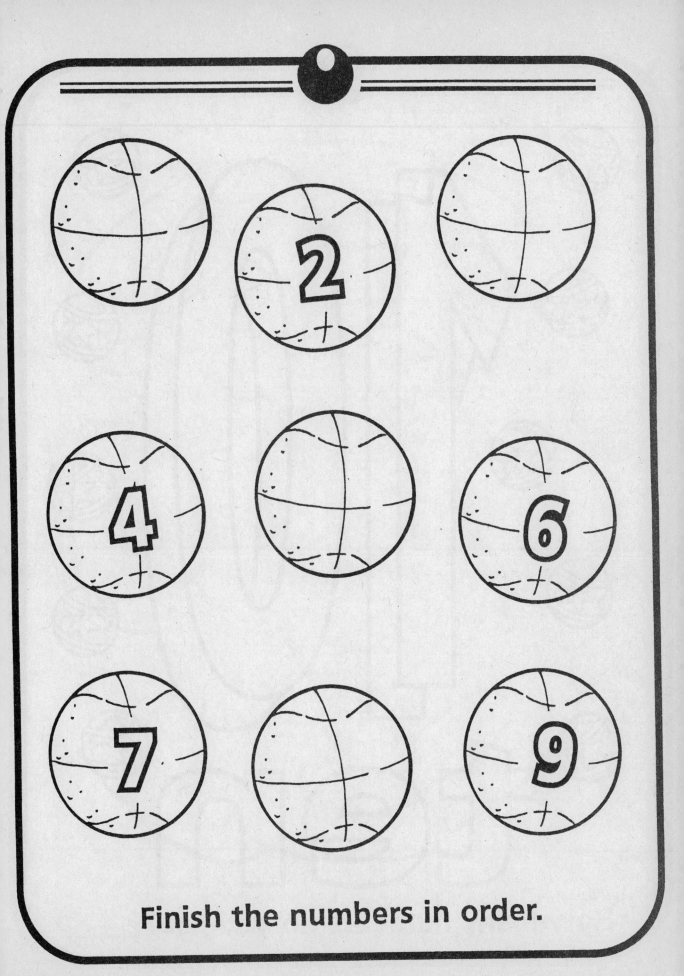

Finish the numbers in order.

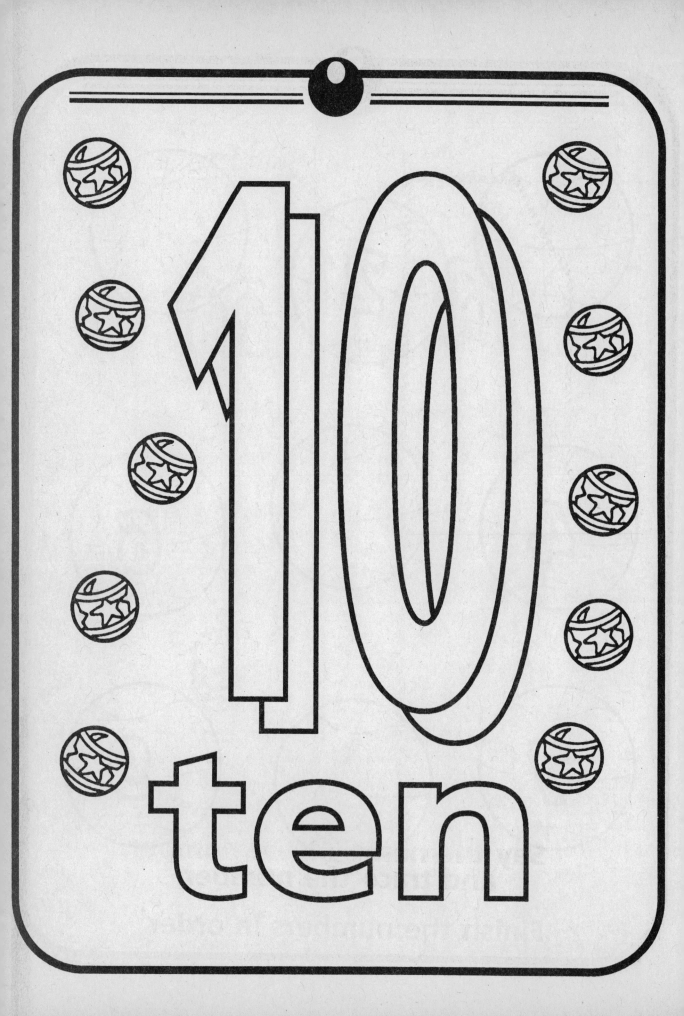

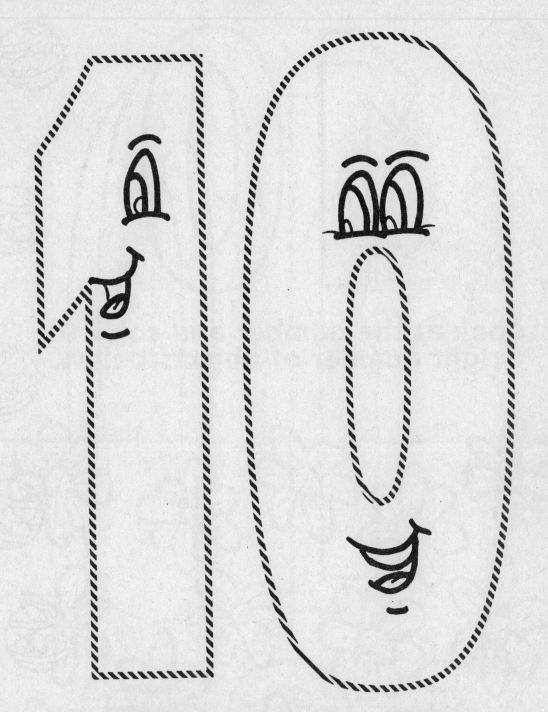

Say the name of the number and trace the number.

10

Look at the number and color the right number of objects below.

Addition

10 + 1 = 11

10 + 2 = ___

10 + 3 = ___

10 + 4 = ___

10 + 5 = ___

10 + 6 = ___

10 + 7 = ___

10 + 8 = ___

10 + 9 = ___

10 + 10 = ___

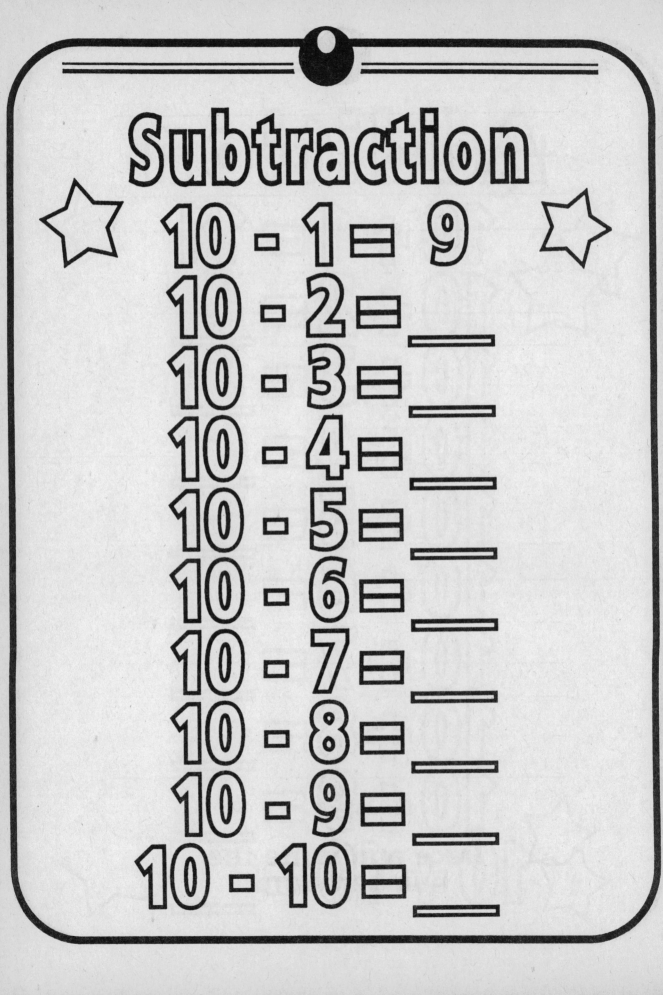

Subtraction

10 - 1 = 9

10 - 2 =

10 - 3 =

10 - 4 =

10 - 5 =

10 - 6 =

10 - 7 =

10 - 8 =

10 - 9 =

10 - 10 =

ten

**Trace and write the
number word.**

Draw two coins for the bank.

1 3 5 6 7 9

Fill in the missing numbers.

5, 6, 7

Circle the right number above.

5

6

7

**Draw a line from each number
to the correct number of objects.**

Draw six ballons.

Draw five fish swimming.

8, 9, 10

Circle the right number above.